WE ARE AWESOME, SO LET'S WRITE ABOUT IT
A Mother and Son Back-and-Forth Journal

_____

(son's name)

_____

(mother's name)

WE ARE AWESOME, SO LET'S WRITE ABOUT IT
A Mother and Son Back-and-Forth Journal

By Hilary Weeks
& Shannon Foster

Printed in the United States of America
Alexanders Printing, Lindon, Utah

TABLE OF CONTENTS

TABLE OF CONTENTS

PURPOSE OF THIS JOURNAL

This journal is designed to help mothers and sons share, laugh, love, bond, and teach each other. As you pass this journal back and forth and fill each page, you will create a history and record that is a true treasure! Go ahead! Just start writing, doodling, coloring, and sharing. You are awesome... so write about it!

WHO WROTE THIS BOOK?

Hilary Weeks grew up in Anchorage, Alaska in a home where her musical talents were supported and encouraged. At age 26, Hilary released her first Christian inspirational CD and has gone on to write and release a total of 11 CDs. Her last three albums each charted in the top ten on the Christian billboard charts. Hilary is the author of several books and finds inspiration in words. She loves spending time with her husband and four daughters and is a big fan of coconut ice cream with raspberries.

Shannon Foster (a.k.a. The Red Headed Hostess) is a mother to one daughter and has a son on the way. She taught LDS seminary for 13 years where she learned to truly love teaching and connecting with youth. She started www.theredheadedhostess.com in order to help others teach the gospel of Jesus Christ to their families. She loves being with her family, teaching, graphic design, and traveling the world.

FUN & USEFUL IDEAS

1- Start at the beginning and work through this book one page at a time, passing the journal back and forth after completing each page.

2- Or pick any page to write on and leave a bookmark where you just finished writing, so when you pass it on the other person knows where to look!

3- Choose a spot where the two of you can leave the journal once you have completed a page (each other's pillow, a desk, a dresser..., just choose a spot and surprise each other with newly filled pages).

4- If you find that you have a lot to say on a particular page, just find some small note pages or cut paper to fit inside your journal, and keep writing! Then just slip your paper in next to the page you filled up and tape it along the top or side of the page.

5- Throughout this book are pages titled "Both of Us". Both mother and son should write on these pages.

6- There are either "Both of Us" pages or pages with "Son" or "Mother" at the top. If "Son" is at the top, then the son should write on that page. Likewise, if "Mother" is at the top, then the mother should write on that page.

Note from Hilary

My mom gave me my first journal (back then we called it a "diary" which has an air of the dramatic) on my eighth birthday. I started writing and haven't stopped. My definition of journaling has changed and adapted through the years. One of my favorite adaptations is journaling I share with my daughters. We write funny, thoughtful, meaningful, silly and love-filled messages and pass them back and forth, leaving them on pillows, computer keyboards, and bathroom counters. From the first sentiment, those journals have become treasures and I know this book will become the same for you.

LOVE,

Hilary Weeks

Note from Shannon

This journal is designed to help strengthen the bond between mother and son by including prompts and subjects that are meaningful and fun, with topics that can help you strengthen and fortify each other. Often as we write, we find words and thoughts that might not have been communicated in a verbal conversation. My hope is that this journal will help you fill each other with words of love and counsel that will bless your lives in immeasurable ways.

LOVE,

Shannon Foster

10

THINGS
I LOVE ABOUT YOU, MOM

1-

2-

3-

4-

5-

6-

7-

8-

9-

10-

10

THINGS
I LOVE ABOUT YOU, SON

1-

2-

3-

4-

5-

6-

7-

8-

9-

10-

BOTH OF US

FUNNY STUFF

 **EEEW!**

Something that always grosses me out:

 EEEW!

Something that always grosses me out:

AAH!

One of my irrational fears is:

AAH!

One of my irrational fears is:

UHH!

One of my pet peeves is:

UHH!

One of my pet peeves is:

_____ SON _____

IF I HAD AN AFTERNOON TO SPEND DOING

ANYTHING I WANTED,

I WOULD...

If I had an afternoon
to spend doing
ANYTHING I WANTED,
I would...

SON

HERE IS A LIST
OF SOME OF **MY** FAVORITE
THINGS

Mother ♥♥♥

HERE IS A LIST
OF SOME OF MY FAVORITE
things
xoxo

SON

SOME THINGS THAT ARE GOING ON IN MY LIFE ARE...

Mother
♥ ♥ ♥

some things
THAT ARE GOING ON
IN MY LIFE ARE...

_____ SON _____

ONE OF MY FAVORITE
SCRIPTURES
(AND WHY I LOVE IT)

ONE OF MY
Favorite
scriptures

(AND WHY I LOVE IT)

SON:
PASTE A RECENT PICTURE
THAT YOU TOOK OF YOUR
MOTHER, AND PASTE
IT HERE.

A RECENT PICTURE I TOOK OF YOU, MOM

SON: What I remember about this moment:

MOTHER: What I remember about this moment:

16

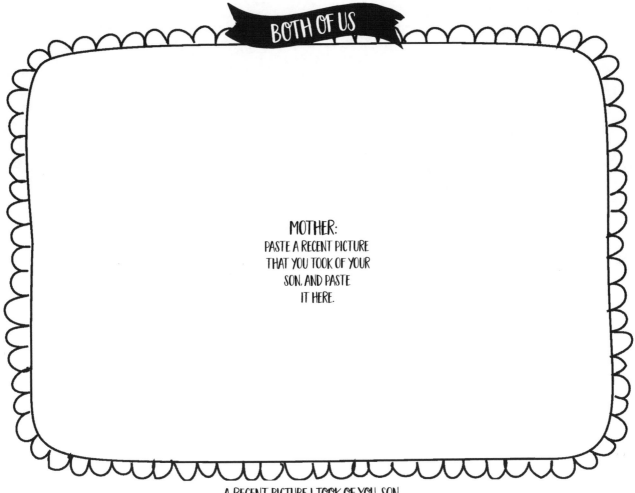

BOTH OF US

MOTHER:
PASTE A RECENT PICTURE
THAT YOU TOOK OF YOUR
SON, AND PASTE
IT HERE.

A RECENT PICTURE I TOOK OF YOU, SON

MOTHER: What I remember about this moment:

SON: What I remember about this moment:

ONE OF THE
BEST THINGS
I HAVE EVER DONE IS:
○ ○ ○ ○ ○ ○ ○ ○ ○ ○
(AND WHY IT WAS SO GREAT)

ONE OF THE
BEST THINGS
I have ever done is:
(AND WHY IT WAS SO GREAT)

I FEEL LIKE TELLING YOU ABOUT:

—————————————— Mother ——————————————
♥ ♥ ♥

today

I FEEL LIKE
TELLING YOU ABOUT:

>>>>>>>>>>>>>>>>>>>>

WHAT I HOPE MY

FUTURE WIFE

>>>>>> IS LIKE: >>>>>>

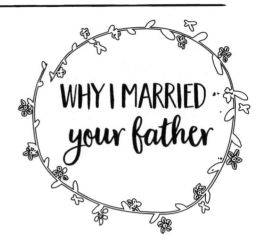

WHY I MARRIED ..
your father

Just Married

SOME GOALS I HAVE ARE:

THINGS I LOVE

MY FAVORITE MOVIES:

SON:	Mother:

MY FAVORITE THINGS TO EAT FOR BREAKFAST:

SON:	Mother:

MY FAVORITE TREATS:

SON:	Mother:

BOTH OF US

OUR BUCKET LISTS

(15 THINGS I WANT TO DO WITH YOU)

SON

1-
2-
3-
4-
5-
6-
7-
8-
9-
10-
11-
12-
13-
14-
15-

MOTHER

1-
2-
3-
4-
5-
6-
7-
8-
9-
10-
11-
12-
13-
14-
15-

SOME OF THE BEST
ADVICE
I HAVE EVER BEEN GIVEN IS:

Mother
♥ ♥ ♥

SOME OF THE BEST
ADVICE
I HAVE EVER BEEN GIVEN IS...

HERE IS A QUOTE
THAT I LOVE
(AND WHY I LOVE IT)

HERE IS A
quote
THAT I LOVE
(AND WHY I LOVE IT)

TEACHERS
I HAVE HAD THAT IMPACTED MY LIFE:
(AND WHAT THEY TAUGHT ME)

Mother
♥ ♥ ♥

Teachers
I HAVE HAD THAT
IMPACTED MY LIFE:

(AND WHAT THEY TAUGHT ME)

IF I COULD BE

INVISIBLE

FOR A DAY, I WOULD...

Mother
♥ ♥ ♥

IF I COULD BE

invisible

FOR A DAY, I WOULD...

35

BOTH OF US

SON
DRAW A SCRIBBLE

Mother,
MAKE HIS SCRIBBLE
INTO A PICTURE

Mother,
DRAW A SCRIBBLE

SON
MAKE HER SCRIBBLE
INTO A PICTURE

IF I COULD
TRAVEL IN TIME,
I WOULD GO AND SEE...
>>>>>>

IF I COULD
TRAVEL IN TIME,
I WOULD GO AND SEE...

MY
FAVORITE AGE
SO FAR HAS BEEN....
(AND HERE IS WHY)

Mother
♥ ♥ ♥

MY
FAVORITE AGE
SO FAR HAS BEEN....
(AND HERE IS WHY)

_____ SON _____

ONE OF MY
FUNNIEST
MEMORIES IN LIFE IS:

ONE OF MY

FUNNIEST

MEMORIES IN LIFE IS:

THE MOST
COURAGEOUS
THING I HAVE EVER DONE IS:

☆ ☆ ☆ ☆ ☆ ☆

THE MOST
COURAGEOUS
THING i HAVE EVER DONE IS:

☆ ☆ ☆ ☆ ☆ ☆

THREE WAYS
THAT WE ARE DIFFERENT

SON
HOW I AM DIFFERENT FROM YOU, MOM

1—

2—

3—

MOTHER
HOW I AM DIFFERENT FROM YOU, SON

1—

2—

3—

46

THREE WAYS
THAT WE ARE THE SAME

SON

HOW I AM THE SAME AS YOU. MOM

1-

2-

3-

MOTHER

HOW I AM THE SAME AS YOU. SON

1-

2-

3-

SON

IF I WERE TO DESCRIBE YOU

TO SOMEONE, I WOULD TELL THEM...

48

Mother
♥ ♥ ♥

IF I WERE TO
Describe
YOU
TO SOMEONE, I WOULD TELL THEM...

49

SON

WHAT I WOULD DO IF I
KNEW
I COULD NOT
FAIL:

WHAT I WOULD DO IF I
KNEW
I COULD NOT
FAIL:

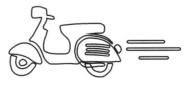

TIMES I HAVE FELT
DIRECTED
BY
Heavenly
Father

52

TIMES I HAVE FELT
Directed
BY
Heavenly
Father

TODAY

I FEEL LIKE
TELLING YOU ABOUT:

Today
I FEEL LIKE
TELLING YOU ABOUT:

THINGS I WANT TO DO

PLACES I WANT TO VISIT:

SON:

Mother:

SKILLS / TALENTS I WANT TO DEVELOP:

SON:

Mother:

PEOPLE I WOULD LIKE TO MEET:

SON:

Mother:

BOTH OF US

IF / THEN

Each of you can write 3 "if" statements (for example: "If you could buy anything in the world..."), and then the other person answers it with a "then" statement (for example: "Then I would buy that cabin we visited last summer.").

SON: **IF**   Mother: **THEN**

1-	
2-	
3-	

Mother: **IF**   SON: **THEN**

1-	
2-	
3-	

MY FAVORITE

TOYS & MEMORIES

AS A CHILD ARE:

MY FAVORITE
TOYS
& MEMORIES
AS A CHILD ARE:

WHAT A TYPICAL
SCHOOL DAY
IS LIKE FOR ME:

CLASSES I TAKE...
FRIENDS I HANG OUT WITH...
THINGS I DO, SEE, HEAR...

Mother
♥ ♥ ♥

WHAT A
typical day
IS LIKE FOR ME:

SOMETHING I FEEL LIKE
WRITING ABOUT
TODAY
IS...

Mother
♥ ♥ ♥

SOMETHING I FEEL LIKE
WRITING ABOUT
today
IS...

SON

DRAW A
TIMELINE
OF THE
most important
& memorable
EVENTS IN YOUR LIFE

BORN

NOW

Mother
♥ ♥ ♥

DRAW A
TIMELINE
OF THE
MOST IMPORTANT
& MEMORABLE
EVENTS IN YOUR LIFE

BORN   NOW

10 qualities
I ADMIRE IN YOU, MOM

1-

2-

3-

4-

5-

6-

7-

8-

9-

10-

10 QUALITIES
I ADMIRE IN YOU, SON

1-

2-

3-

4-

5-

6-

7-

8-

9-

10-

FINISH THESE SENTENCES

SOME THINGS IN THE WORLD THAT I WOULD LIKE TO SEE ARE...

SON:

Mother:

I WOULD LIKE TO BE AN EXPERT IN...

SON:

Mother:

IF I HAD TO EAT THE SAME THING FOR ONE MONTH, IT WOULD BE...

SON:

Mother:

SOMETHING VALUABLE
I LEARNED RECENTLY:

SOMETHING
valuable
I LEARNED RECENTLY:

MOM, IF I COULD BUY YOU

ANY 10 THINGS

THEY WOULD BE:

1-

2-

3-

4-

5-

6-

7-

8-

9-

10-

1-

2-

3-

4-

5-

6-

7-

8-

9-

10-

SON, IF I COULD BUY YOU

ANY 10 THINGS

THEY WOULD BE:

_____ SON _____

THREE THINGS

THAT I **KNOW** ARE TRUE...

_____ SON _____

TODAY

I FEEL LIKE
TELLING YOU ABOUT:

Mother
♥ ♥ ♥

...•••❀❀❀•••...

TODAY
I FEEL LIKE
TELLING YOU ABOUT:

...•••❀❀❀•••...

BOTH OF US

MOM,

ONE QUESTION I HAVE
ALWAYS WANTED TO
ASK YOU IS:

SON,

HERE IS MY ANSWER:

SON,

ONE QUESTION I HAVE
ALWAYS WANTED TO
ASK YOU IS:

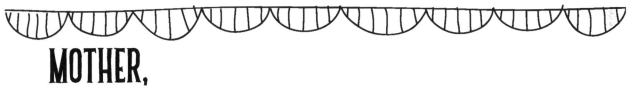

MOTHER,

HERE IS MY ANSWER:

SON

THE
HARDEST
THING

IN MY LIFE RIGHT NOW IS...

THE HARDEST THING IN MY LIFE RIGHT NOW IS...

WHO MY
BEST FRIENDS
ARE:

(AND WHY THEY ARE MY BEST FRIENDS)

WHO MY
BEST FRIENDS
ARE:
(AND WHY THEY ARE MY BEST FRIENDS)

I AM
GRATEFUL FOR:

Mother
♥ ♥ ♥

(LITTLE)
THINGS ABOUT
TODAY
I AM
GRATEFUL FOR:

MY
FAVORITE
FAMILY TRADITIONS
ARE...

Mother
♥ ♥ ♥

MY
favorite
FAMILY TRADITIONS
ARE...

PHRASES THAT REMIND ME OF...

WHAT MEMORIES ARE YOU REMINDED OF WHEN YOU SEE THESE SIX PHRASES? CHOOSE ONE OF THE PHRASES, CIRCLE IT, AND WRITE ABOUT THAT MEMORY IN THE SPACE BELOW.

"THE BIG GAME"   "YOU FELL ASLEEP"
"AT THE BEACH"   "YOU WERE SO SCARED"
"YOU LAUGHED SO HARD"   "IN THE YARD"

SON:

Mother:

PHRASES THAT REMIND ME OF...

WHAT MEMORIES ARE YOU REMINDED OF WHEN YOU SEE THESE SIX PHRASES? CHOOSE ONE OF THE PHRASES, CIRCLE IT, AND WRITE ABOUT THAT MEMORY IN THE SPACE BELOW.

"A FILTHY MESS"   "EARLY IN THE MORNING"
"AT THE STORE"   "THE FIRST TIME YOU..."
"IN THE MOUNTAINS"   "YOUR FACE SAID IT ALL"

SON:

Mother:

HERE IS A
SCRIPTURE
THAT GIVES ME
STRENGTH
(AND WHY IT HELPS ME)

SON

HERE IS A
SCRIPTURE
THAT GIVES ME
STRENGTH
(AND WHY IT HELPS ME)

WHEN I
GROW UP,
I WANT TO...

BE...

HAVE...

BE LIKE...

GO...

DO...

90

WHAT I HAVE
LEARNED
ABOUT
GROWING UP:

- -

WHAT I
IMAGINE
YOU BEING LIKE WHEN YOU
GROW UP:

IF I COULD PLAN OUR NEXT
FAMILY VACATION,
WE WOULD:

————————— Mother —————————
♥ ♥ ♥

IF I COULD PLAN OUR NEXT
FAMILY VACATION,
WE WOULD:

I FEEL
CLOSE TO
GOD
WHEN...

I FEEL
close to
GOD
WHEN...

THINGS I LOVE

MY FAVORITE HOMEMADE MEALS:

SON:	Mother:

MY FAVORITE THINGS IN NATURE:

SON:	Mother:

MY FAVORITE PLACES TO SHOP:

SON:	Mother:

MORE FAVORITES!

5 OF MY FAVORITE BOOKS

SON...
1–
2–
3–
4–
5–

Mom...
1–
2–
3–
4–
5–

5 OF MY FAVORITE RESTAURANTS

SON...
1–
2–
3–
4–
5–

Mom...
1–
2–
3–
4–
5–

HERE IS A LIST OF
MY FAVORITE THINGS ABOUT:

WINTER

SPRING

SUMMER

FALL

Here is a list of
MY FAVORITE THINGS ABOUT:

Winter

Spring

Summer

Fall

SON

TODAY
I FEEL LIKE
TELLING YOU
ABOUT:

100

Mother
♥ ♥ ♥

Today
I FEEL LIKE
TELLING YOU ABOUT:

A FAVORITE
MEMORY
I HAVE OF US:

Mother

♥ ♥ ♥

A FAVORITE **MEMORY** I HAVE OF US:

xoxo

SON

WHAT I HAVE LEARNED ABOUT
PRAYER

Mother
♥ ♥ ♥

WHAT I HAVE LEARNED ABOUT
prayer

SON:
PASTE A FUNNY PICTURE
THAT RECENTLY HAPPENED
WITH YOU AND OTHER
MEMBERS OF YOUR FAMILY

SON: What I remember about this moment:

MOTHER: What I remember about this moment:

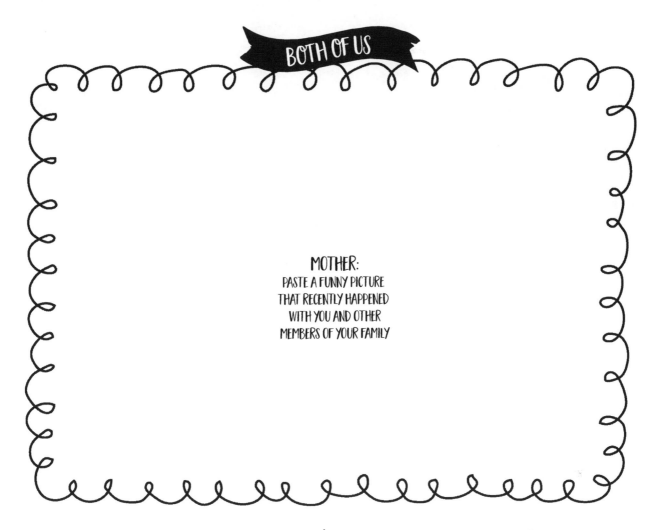

BOTH OF US

MOTHER:
PASTE A FUNNY PICTURE
THAT RECENTLY HAPPENED
WITH YOU AND OTHER
MEMBERS OF YOUR FAMILY

MOTHER: What I remember about this moment:

SON: What I remember about this moment:

HERE IS A FLOOR PLAN
OF MY
DREAM HOME:

Mother
♥ ♥ ♥

HERE IS A FLOOR PLAN
OF MY
DREAM HOME:

WHAT I KNOW ABOUT
Heavenly Father

WHAT I KNOW ABOUT
Heavenly
Father

——————————— SON ———————————

SOME OF MY
HEROES
ARE

—————————— **Mother** ——————————
♥ ♥ ♥

SOME OF MY
Heroes
ARE:

✿ ✿ ✿ ✿

SOMETHING I FEEL LIKE
TELLING YOU
ABOUT TODAY..

Mother
♥ ♥ ♥

SOMETHING I FEEL LIKE
TELLING YOU
ABOUT TODAY..

ONE WORD

WHAT FAMILY MEMORY COMES TO MIND WHEN YOU SEE THESE SINGLE WORDS?

WATER

SON:

Mother:

TIRED

SON:

Mother:

SACRED

SON:

Mother:

116

BOTH OF US

MORE FAVORITES!

5 OF MY FAVORITE THINGS TO DO

SON:

1–

2–

3–

4–

5–

Mom...

1–

2–

3–

4–

5–

5 OF MY FAVORITE PLACES I HAVE BEEN

SON:

1–

2–

3–

4–

5–

Mom...

1–

2–

3–

4–

5–

SON

SOME IMPORTANT

CHOICES

I STILL HAVE AHEAD OF ME ARE:

>>>>>>>>>>>>>>>>>>>>>>>>>>>>

Mother
♥ ♥ ♥

SOME IMPORTANT
choices
YOU STILL HAVE
AHEAD OF YOU ARE:

THINGS THAT MAKE ME **HAPPY** ARE:

Mother
♥ ♥ ♥

THINGS THAT MAKE ME
HAPPY
ARE:

THREE WORDS
THAT I WANT TO
DESCRIBE ME:
(AND WHY)

1-

2-

3-

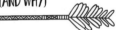

THREE WORDS
THAT I WANT TO
DESCRIBE ME:
(AND WHY)

1-

2-

3-

SON

SOME OF MY
LIFE DREAMS
ARE:

Mother
♥ ♥ ♥

SOME OF MY
LIFE
Dreams
ARE:

FINISH THESE SENTENCES

I WISH I NEVER AGAIN HAD TO...

SON:

Mother:

I REALLY HOPE THAT...

SON:

Mother:

I AM ALWAYS GRATEFUL WHEN YOU...

SON:

Mother:

ONE WORD

WHAT FAMILY MEMORY COMES TO MIND WHEN YOU SEE THESE SINGLE WORDS?

MESSY

SON:	Mother:

COLD

SON:	Mother:

MIRACLE

SON:	Mother:

_____ SON _____

PEOPLE IN OUR
NEIGHBORHOOD & FAMILY
I ADMIRE
(AND WHY)

Mother

♥ ♥ ♥

PEOPLE IN OUR
NEIGHBORHOOD & FAMILY
I ADMIRE
(AND WHY)

SON

SOME THINGS IN MY
NEAR FUTURE
I AM...

EXCITED ABOUT:

NERVOUS ABOUT:

PREPARING FOR:

DREADING:

130

SOME THINGS IN MY

★ **NEAR FUTURE** ★

★ I AM... ★

EXCITED ABOUT:

NERVOUS ABOUT:

PREPARING FOR:

DREADING:

MY FAVORITE THINGS TO

DO

(FILL THE PAGE WITH ALL
OF YOUR FAVORITE PERSONAL
TIME ACTIVITIES)

Mother
♥ ♥ ♥

MY FAVORITE THINGS TO
Do

(FILL THE PAGE WITH ALL OF YOUR FAVORITE PERSONAL TIME ACTIVITIES)

_____ SON _____

WHAT I IMAGINE
HEAVEN
TO BE LIKE:

WHAT I IMAGINE

Heaven

TO BE LIKE:

FINISH THESE SENTENCES

IF I COULD HAVE ANY SUPER POWER, IT WOULD BE...

SON:

Mother:

MY THREE MOST CHERISHED ITEMS I OWN ARE...

SON:

Mother:

THE CRAZIEST THING I HAVE EVER DONE IS...

SON:

Mother:

BOTH OF US

THINGS I LEARNED
ABOUT YOU (MOM) FROM THIS JOURNAL

1-

2-

3-

4-

5-

6-

7-

8-

9-

10-

THINGS I LEARNED
ABOUT YOU (SON) FROM THIS JOURNAL

1-

2-

3-

4-

5-

6-

7-

8-

9-

10-

A FAILURE

I HAVE HAD THAT HAS TURNED INTO

A GREAT BLESSING:

A FAILURE
I HAVE HAD THAT HAS TURNED INTO
A GREAT BLESSING:

SON

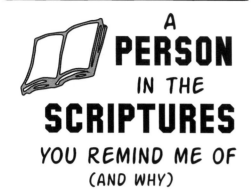

A PERSON IN THE SCRIPTURES

YOU REMIND ME OF
(AND WHY)

A PERSON
IN THE SCRIPTURES
YOU REMIND ME OF
(AND WHY)

SON

MOM,

DON'T FORGET...

142

Mother
♥ ♥ ♥

SON,
DON'T FORGET...

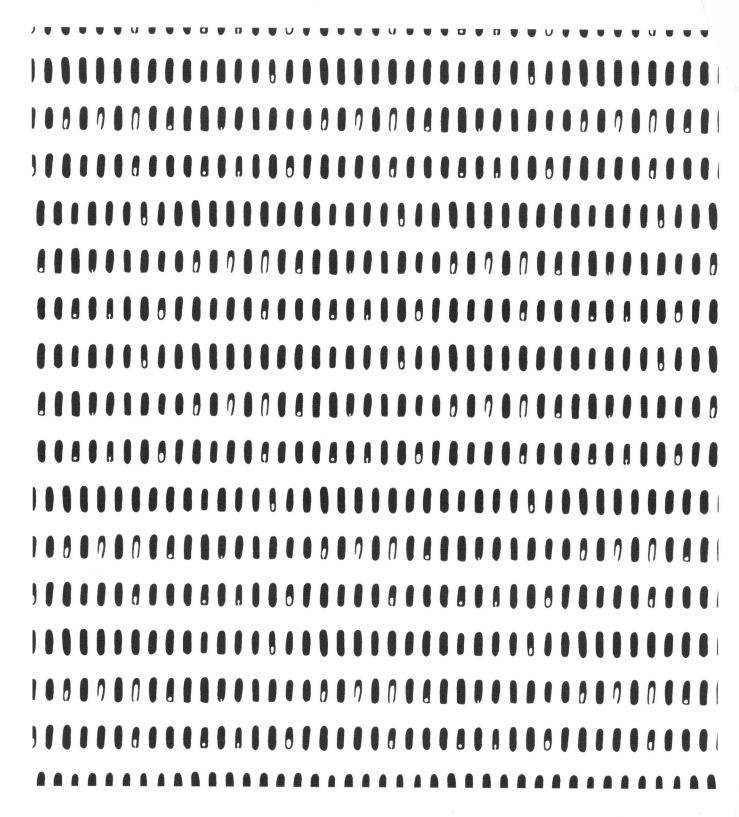

34352348R00080

Made in the USA
Columbia, SC
14 November 2018